Feathers

by Jennifer Boothroyd

Lerner Publications Company · Minneapolis

Feathers are light body parts.

Birds are covered with feathers.

Feathers grow from a bird's **skin**.

Soft and fluffy feathers keep birds warm.

Feathers used for flying are strong.

They help keep birds moving in the air.

Ducks have feathers that help them float.

Some birds have fancy feathers.

Feathers are many colors.

Some feathers change color in different seasons.

11

Some birds take baths in water to clean their feathers.

Other birds clean their feathers with their **beaks**.

Birds pull out old or broken feathers.

They also **shed** feathers.

Feathers can help birds hide.

Feathers help birds **survive** in their surroundings.

Feathers

Feathers used for flying are strong. Each feather connects to the bird's skin at the quill. The rachis is a hollow tube. It is in the center of the feather. Barbs branch out from each side. These make the vane of the feather. On each barb are tiny barbules. The barbules hook together. This makes the feather smooth and stiff.

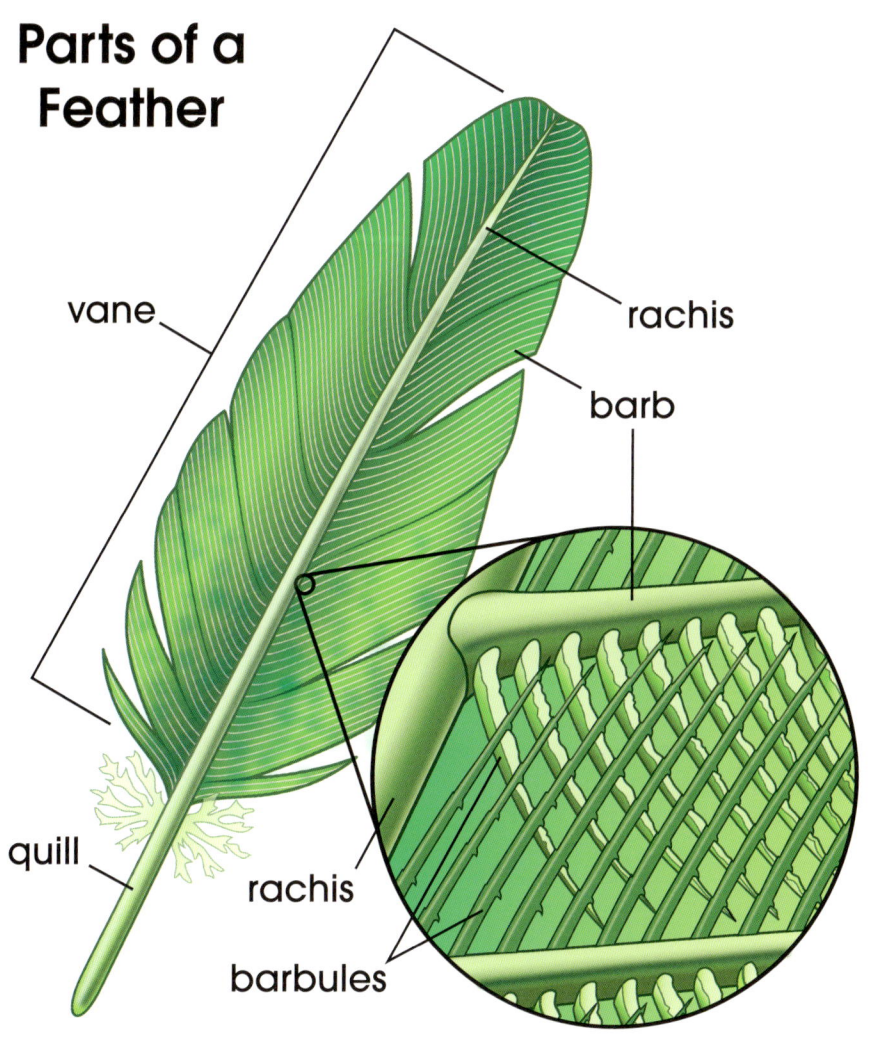

Facts about Feathers

 People need special permission to collect bald eagle feathers.

 Feathers are made of keratin. Human fingernails are made of the same material.

 For centuries, people used feather quills for writing with ink.

 In many kinds of birds, the male has more colorful feathers than the female.

 The feathers of flamingos change color depending on what they eat.

 A penguin has short feathers. They are very close together. They keep water away from the penguin's skin.

 Some humming birds have fewer than 1,000 feathers. Some swans have more that 25,000.

Glossary

 **beaks** – the hard mouthparts of birds

 **feathers** – light body parts that cover a bird's skin

 **shed** – to lose or fall off

 **skin** – the outer covering of a person or animal

 **survive** – to keep living

Index

clean – 12–13

colors – 10–11

float – 8

flying – 6

shed – 15

skin – 4

survive – 17

Copyright © 2012 by Lerner Publishing Group, Inc.

All rights reserved. International copyright secured. No part of this book may be reproduced, stored in a retrieval system, or transmitted in any form or by any means—electronic, mechanical, photocopying, recording, or otherwise—without the prior written permission of Lerner Publishing Group, Inc., except for the inclusion of brief quotations in an acknowledged review.

The images in this book are used with the permission of: © Adrianna Williams/CORBIS, pp. 2, 22 (second from top); © Gunter Marx Photography/CORBIS, p. 3; © Mike Neale/Dreamstime.com, pp. 4, 22 (fourth from top); © Philippe Clement/Minden Pictures, p. 5; © Bryant Aardema/Shutterstock Images, p. 6; © Marty Ellis/Shutterstock Images, p. 7; © Keith Douglas/CORBIS, p. 8; © Konrad Wothe/Minden Pictures, p. 9; © Harry Giglio/Bluemoon Stock/Photolibrary, p. 10; © Robert Maier/Animals Animals, p. 11 (left); © Jim Brandenburg/Minden Pictures, p. 11 (right); © Gordon & Cathy Illg/Animals Animals, p. 12; © Fiona Green, p. 13; © Juergen & Christine Sohns/Animals Animals, pp. 14, 22 (top); © Doug Cheeseman/Peter Arnold, Inc./Alamy, pp. 15, 22 (third from top); © SMuller/Wildlife/Photolibrary, p. 16; © Arthur Morris/Visuals Unlimited, Inc., pp. 17, 22 (bottom); © Laura Westlund/Independent Picture Service, p. 19.
Front Cover: © Marty Ellis/Shutterstock Images.

Main body text set in ITC Avant Garde Gothic 21/25. Typeface provided by Adobe Systems.

Lerner Publications Company
A division of Lerner Publishing Group, Inc.
241 First Avenue North
Minneapolis, MN 55401 U.S.A.

Website address: www.lernerbooks.com

Library of Congress Cataloging-in-Publication Data

Boothroyd, Jennifer, 1972–
    Feathers / by Jennifer Boothroyd.
      p. cm. — (First step nonfiction — Body coverings)
    Includes index.
    ISBN 978–0–7613–5785–8 (lib. bdg. : alk. paper)
    1. Feathers—Juvenile literature. I. Title.
QL697.4.B66 2012
598.147—dc22   2010050648

Manufactured in the United States of America
1 – PC – 7/15/11